The Bill of Rights

What It Is, What It Means, and How It's Been Misused

BY SHANNON LEIGH FALLON

DICKENS PRESS
IRVINE, CALIFORNIA

Copyright 1996 by Shannon L. Fallon

Published by Dickens Press
P.O. Box 4289
Irvine, CA 92716
(800) 230-8158

All rights reserved. No part of this book may be used or reproduced by any means, electronic, mechanical, photocopying, recording, or other, without written permission except in the case of brief quotations for use in articles and reviews.

All information in this book is given without guarantees on the part of the author or publisher, and the author and publisher disclaim all liability in connection with the implementation of this information. Every effort has been made to make this book as authentic and accurate as possible.

Library of Congress Cataloging-in-Publication Data

Fallon, Shannon Leigh, 1970-
   The Bill of Rights: what it is, what it means, and how it's been misused / by Shannon Leigh Fallon.
     p. cm.
   Includes index.
   ISBN 1-880741-25-3
   1. Civil rights—United States—Interpretation and construction.
2. United States—Constitutional law—Amendments—1st-10th—
Interpretation and construction.   I. Title.
KF4750.F27 1995
342.73'083--dc20
[347.30285]   95-38409
                                                                                  CIP

Distributed to the trade by National Book Network, Inc.
ISBN: 1-880741-25-3
Printed in the United States of America on acid-free paper
10 9 8 7 6 5 4 3 2 1
First printing 1995

Interior and cover design © 1996 Michele Lanci-Altomare
Cover illustration © 1996 Guadalupe Hernandez
Edited by Gina Misiroglu

To my publisher, who has been like a mother to me.

Contents

Acknowledgments • vii
Introduction • ix

RIGHTS 1
A BRIEF HISTORY 11
THE FIRST AMENDMENT 19
THE SECOND AMENDMENT 24
THE THIRD AMENDMENT 30
THE FOURTH AMENDMENT 33
THE FIFTH AMENDMENT 37
THE SIXTH AMENDMENT 43
THE SEVENTH AMENDMENT 48
THE EIGHTH AMENDMENT 51
THE NINTH AMENDMENT 58
THE TENTH AMENDMENT 63
AMENDMENTS 11 THROUGH 27 69

Index • 83
About the Author • 86

ACKNOWLEDGMENTS

I WOULD FIRST LIKE TO THANK MY PUBLISHER, DICKENS PRESS, for entrusting me to write a book on the most important document in American history. I would also like to extend my gratitude to Gina Misiroglu, who not only helped me "draw within the lines," but also shared with me the idea that the most compelling books are those which strive to be objective. Thanks to Michele Lanci-Altomare for designing the cover and interior, and Guadalupe Hernandez, who created a cover illustration that couldn't have been closer to the image in my mind. I'd like to thank Tibor Machan, author and professor of philosophy at Auburn University, who reviewed my initial manuscript for content, and for waking me up to an early morning insight. I must acknowledge my parents, who taught me at a very young age the value of personal responsibility, and for respecting my privacy even as a pubescent adolescent. My siblings Tara and James too deserve my thanks for challenging me with their own legal and philosophical interpretations of freedom. I am, of course, forever indebted to the Founding Fathers of this country—truly the wisest and most courageous group of men who ever lived. Finally, my sincerest love and thanks are reserved for my husband, Paul, whose unending inspiration and support could make a rock smile any day.

INTRODUCTION

REMEMBER U.S. GOVERNMENT IN HIGH SCHOOL? REMEMBER learning about the Articles of Confederation, the Declaration of Independence, the Constitution, and the Bill of Rights? Me neither.

I recently picked up my old American government book, still covered with the mandatory brown paper book cover, and scanned through it. I found myself interested for the first time. As I read, I began to notice a continuous theme, a context from which I could see American history evolving. It wasn't the interrupted, discontinuous flow of information I (didn't) remember from high school. What I noticed was that history did not have a beginning or an end, and that everything that happened was a process, building upon itself throughout space and time. There were reasons that things happened. U.S. presidents didn't elect themselves, wars didn't ignite themselves, and prisoners didn't imprison themselves. Something, somewhere, somehow, caused these things to happen. History *moved,* and as I have learned since, never stopped either.

I learned that many of our historical heroes were not angels; some of the new European colonists were a little too rough and tough around the edges, a tad too ethnocentric, a wee bit too greedy, and generally speaking, *not* the kind of people I'd invite to a small dinner party. However, they *were* the kind of people I'd want to protect me and my rights. I learned that in the wake of their sought-after freedom were millions of enslaved or killed persons unable to compete with their race toward freedom. I learned that every new nation and every great individual has a past, and within that past is room for improvement and conjecture. Our founders had a vision of freedom, and they would do what they had to in order to attain that freedom. If it weren't for their courage to break free from a life of ignorance, religious intolerance, and social inequality in their homeland in Europe, I would not be protected under those same freedoms today. Perhaps I wouldn't have the right to write this book. The United States Constitution which they promised America is invaluable. Unlike any other constitution in the world, it was a promise of freedom; a promise to protect the rights and liberties of individuals against the tyranny of anyone who dared to take them away. Like a priceless heirloom, we must treasure and safeguard it.

Rights

No man has a natural right to commit aggression on the equal rights of another; and this is all from which the laws ought to restrain him.

—THOMAS JEFFERSON

$\mathcal{I}$'M A COLLEGE GRADUATE, AND UNTIL I BEGAN WRITING THIS book, I did not know what my individual rights were. Sure, on many occasions throughout my life I had prefaced a demand for something with "I have a right to . . .", assuming I knew what I was talking about. Yet all I was really doing was repeating what I had heard others say, without ever questioning if what I was saying was true or not. I eventually realized that I was not the only one.

Recently, when I told a friend that I was writing a book on the Bill of Rights, she asked, "You mean like 'thou shalt not covet thy neighbor's wife'?" Another friend suggested I include a chapter on women's rights. I even had someone twice my age ask what they were. I was stunned, but not really.

Like millions of other Americans, I began to feel cheated by an educational system that was more concerned with its own nonacademic agenda than teaching me something I would always value. I wished that my teachers had taught about the Constitution in a manner filled with such excitement that I would always remember its importance. Everyday we labored over subjects we knew we'd never use again, yet were promised would someday change our lives.

What I want to know, what I need to learn for myself today, is why I wasn't encouraged to seek out and understand the single most important document in my life as an American—the Bill of Rights. What are my rights as an American? Not as a female, or a heterosexual, or a Caucasian, or even as a chocolate lover, but as an individual engendered with specific, inalienable rights.

A right is defined as a natural or God-given authority received at birth, to act in one's own self-interest with total control over one's life and property as long as others are not injured or their property taken or damaged in the process. A right is something we all share equally, and which does not impose an obligation on someone else to do anything for us in exchange. We don't have, for example, the right to a home, a job, child care, health insurance, a $50,000-a-year income, a Mercedes, or a Monet painting. These are things we may desire or need, and we all have the right to pursue them. We do not, however, have the right to have them; they are not entitlements. In other words, we cannot expect someone else to provide us with these material assets. They must be earned; they are not ours simply by the act of being born. A right is not something granted by government, but is to be protected by government.

We all have the same basic human rights regardless of whether you believe they come from God or the natural order of things. They are the rights to life, liberty, and the pursuit of happiness. That is the basic political philosophy of our founders as expressed in the Declaration of Independence and the Constitution. The Bill of Rights is therefore nothing more than an extension of those basic human rights as expressed and interpreted by the founders. The Bill of Rights is much like any other written document in that it is just as suggestible to different interpretations by different people, regardless of what, for example, the authors (the founders) had intended. Some people read an article or amendment one way, while others are impressed completely differently. There are some who believe that the Constitution should be read literally, without room for others' interpretations, much like a refuge which promises protection from any danger. Others contend that the Constitution is but a guideline, a reference from which the American people can build upon, extrapolate from, and in some cases, even take away. The former might believe, for example, that the First Amendment right to freedom of speech must be protected under all circumstances—that it protects all speech. The latter, on the other hand, might argue that this First Amendment right protects only certain speech, such as that which is not harmful to someone else, and leaves open for speculation and opinion that which advertises, disrespects, or discriminates. Most of the time, these differences in understanding among people are not a problem—in fact they can be healthy—they stimulate public discourse and social change. The purpose of this book is to illuminate some of these different interpretations, and to examine the Constitution from the context in which it was written—why it was written, what was intended, and how it was (hoped) to be interpreted.

So as to facilitate the reader's interpretation, I have structured the book to be as straightforward as possible. Each chapter states the literal definition of the amendment (what it is), an explanation of that definition (what it means), and the ways in which it has been abused (how it is misused today). In most instances, I have also included an example of such misuse. Additionally, I have included a section which addresses a range of interpretation of individual rights. As mentioned earlier, since each amendment is interpreted differently by everyone, a list of several different interpretations might better enable you to not only see the layers of interpretation, but more importantly, illustrate how consistent they are with the literal definition of the amendment (what it is). For example, one person might interpret the Second Amendment's right to bear arms as the right to own any weapon which hangs from one's arm, while another interprets it as the right to own nuclear and semiautomatic weapons. In other words, you will be able to see the difference between the Constitution's definition and the ways people have interpreted it in recent and historic times. Since the founders aren't here to explain exactly what they intended, we can only understand them based on our own world views, our own personal belief systems, and our own social mores. Seemingly, the only way that we can truly minimize the confusion (the misuse) then, is to abide by each of the Bill of Rights' exact words as best we can. The standard of misuse for this book is therefore directly related to how the people and its government have failed to adhere to the amendments' literal meanings.

There are five "zones" of interpretation: two "extreme" interpretations, one common interpretation of "what most people would agree," and two interpretations based on the gray areas in politics, called the "bones of contention." The following bell curve illustrates the range of interpretations for individual rights:

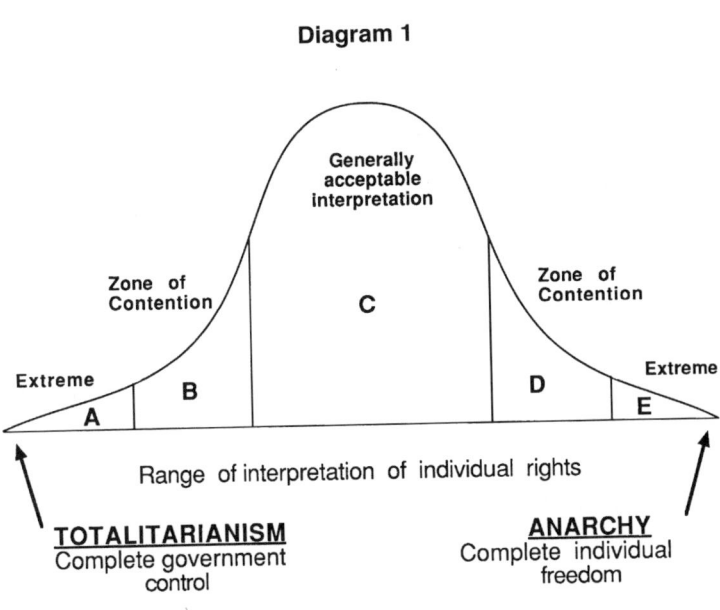

This curve reflects the various ways our rights can be interpreted. Zone C is the broad central region of the curve that reflects the most common, generally accepted interpretation of a right. It is within this region that one might encounter the majority of opinions in America. The majority of Americans, for instance, believe that most narcotics such as LSD and cocaine should remain illegal, while other recreational drugs such as alcohol and tobacco should remain legal. If this was a diagram depicting a political spectrum (though not one which necessarily supports or refutes this particular drug issue), this region would include Republican and Democratic philosophies in a democratic system of government. In other words, most people who live in America would characterize their political views as either Republican or Democrat.

At each end of the curve are the extreme interpretations, reflecting an interpretation based upon the complete subversion of individual rights (zone A), or the complete freedom of individual rights (zone E). A person operating from the extreme A zone might hold the opinion that all drugs, including even medicinal drugs, should be illegal. Conversely, a person operating from the extreme E zone would hold the opinion that all drugs, including LSD and cocaine, should be legalized. In a political spectrum, one might say that zone A reflects totalitarian interpretations (complete government control of individual behavior), whereas zone E reflects anarchistic interpretations (complete freedom of individual behavior).

Between the center and the extremes are the zones of contention, zones B and D ("Bones of contention" in this book), where most of the discourse in our present society is concentrated. An individual representing zone B would hold the opinion that all narcotics, including alcohol and tobacco, should remain illegal, though medicinal drugs should remain legal and available. An individual representing zone D, on the other hand, would believe that most drugs, regardless of their social acceptability, should be legalized. On the political spectrum, zone B might reflect more fascistic and communistic interpretations, where individual freedoms are minimized. Zone D, on the other hand, reflects more of a libertarian slant, where individual freedoms are maximized.

The various interpretations are not necessarily synonymous with political parties and the philosophies they espouse. As described above, they do tend to follow similar interpretive patterns as far as individual rights are concerned. It should be stated that the interpretation of individual rights by different political groups and parties are often given as a linear representation of the political spectrum, as shown below:

Diagram 2

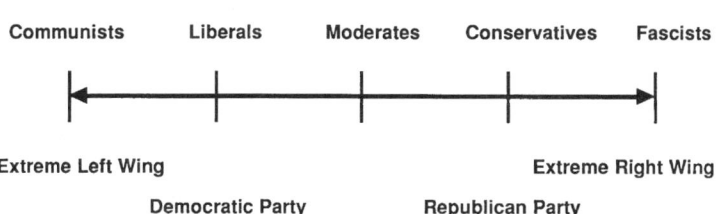

This simple chart reflects what most people understand in contemporary U.S. society, yet it is highly misleading, since it puts two totalitarian forms of government (communism and fascism) at opposite ends of the political spectrum, rather than next to one another, where they really belong, since both are political systems which espouse the restriction of individual rights. A more useful and accurate representation of the political systems, especially with regard to the way they interpret individual rights, is shown below:

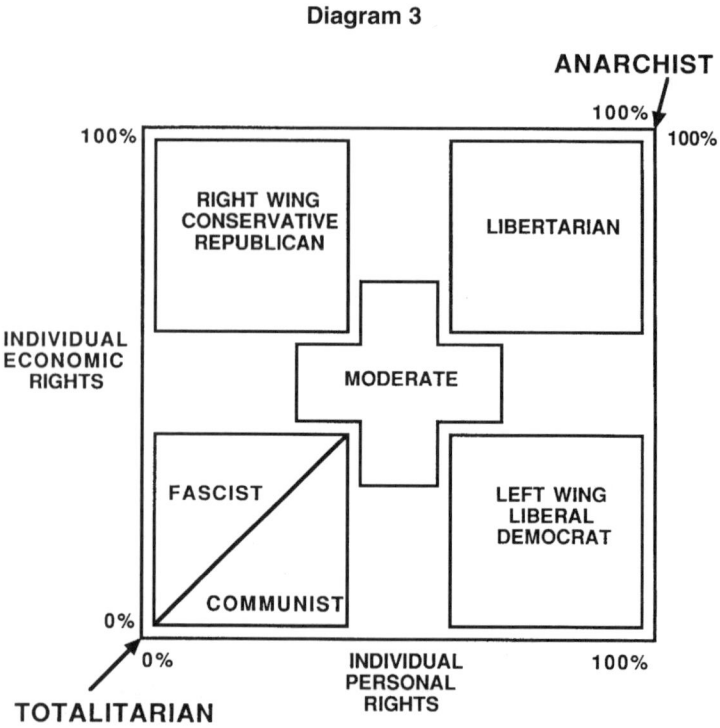

Diagram 3

In this diagram, both forms of *totalitarianism* (fascism and communism) are in the same sphere at the lower left part of the diagram where there are few individual rights. At the opposite end of the spectrum is *libertarianism,* where personal and economic individual rights are maximized. The other common monikers ("moderate," "conservative," and "liberal") in the modern U.S. political system are variations on these themes (although there are some overlaps that are not indicated in this diagram).

Some people would, and do, object to the implications in diagrams 1 and 3. They might ask, "What about the economic, political, and social rights of *groups* rather than *individuals?*" The Bill of Rights does not, however, ensure the rights of groups based on age, gender, sexual orientation, ethnicity, class, region, or ideology. The Bill of Rights is about the rights of individuals, pure and simple. Ensuring the rights of groups would appear to be arbitrary and divisive, and would ultimately destroy individual rights, since group rights will always manifest themselves in the form of *special* rights, whereby the rights of the group are somehow superior to those of individuals. We do, for example, have the right to pursue an education as individuals; we do not, however, have "educational rights" as a mass society. In other words, we do not have the constitutional right as individuals to force others to pay for our education. Individuals today are accepted into colleges and even given scholarships because they are considered to be of a minority status. Similarly, we have the right to be heterosexual, homosexual, or bisexual as individuals; we do not, however, have "heterosexual rights" or "gay rights" according to the Constitution. In other words, we do not have special rights to a job simply because we are heterosexual or homosexual. We have the right to seek health care, but we do not have a constitutional right to demand that someone else pay for it; we do not have "health care rights." Today, people—including illegal immigrants who do not even pay the taxes which support such programs—are given free health care because they cannot afford it. The list of special rights goes on.

Our founders did not provide us with group rights since it would create conflicts of interest among all people; it is for this reason they left Europe in the first place—the rights of certain groups and classes of people were superior to those of all others. Similarly today, the concept of personal responsibility and individual rights are challenged by the misconceived idea that society owes people something. It is for this reason that a firm adherence to the basic principles of the Bill of Rights was, and is, the only way our political system can survive the inevitable challenges by the totalitarian tendencies of government. Yes, even our government.

Before I begin my examination of the Bill of Rights, I believe it is prudent to first provide a brief outline of American history which culminated in the drafting of the Bill of Rights. Without an understanding of why and how it originally came into existence, we cannot fully appreciate its value, not only as an American trademark, but as a living, breathing thing, which could one day become extinct.

A Brief History

History can be well written only in a free country.

—Voltaire

EUROPEAN EXPLORERS FIRST BEGAN THEIR EXPEDITIONS TO THE Americas over 250 years ago because of the simple fact that they weren't satisfied with the social and economic conditions in their own countries. The English were especially frustrated, not only because they couldn't find jobs, but because they were denied the right to express their religious beliefs in the privacy of their own homes. The British Parliament had given them a choice—

they could either accept the official English church, or pretend to.

America seemed like the ideal place to settle. With what appeared to be an infinite supply of land to cultivate and settle upon, and nobody to tell them what they could and could not worship, America was hard to resist. It seemed as though the American ideal of life, liberty, and the pursuit of happiness was rightly attainable even in its infancy; people believed that they were entitled to certain rights before such a concept was even indoctrinated in America.

The first people who attempted to settle in what is now North Carolina had such little luck finding fertile land that they left shortly thereafter. Eventually, after numerous other attempts and failures, some European settlers colonized an area of Virginia they called Jamestown. It would be here, thirty-one years later in 1619, that the first seeds of American democracy were planted. With the exception of the King-appointed governor, the colonists were able to enact their own laws, and established a lawmaking group called the House of Burgesses. The House of Burgesses consisted of twenty-two spokespersons from the surrounding settlements, designated to represent the voices and concerns of the people. Voting rights were established, and judges, justices of the peace, and sheriffs were elected. In other words, the people began to govern themselves. They were on their way.

Then came the many wars over land entitlement. It is not surprising that all Europeans wanted a share of the land, and since not a whole lot was stopping them, they all wanted the largest share possible. Let's face it, they wanted it all; they wanted to own the western lands. By 1750, England, Spain, and France had all claimed land in the Americas. It was at this time that England and France went to war; the winner, it was agreed, would take all. It was also around this time that our first founding father was introduced into American history. His name was George Washington. At age twenty-one, Washington was sent to fight against the French. It was the beginning of the French and Indian War, named after the joint struggle of both the French and the Indians. Apparently, nobody bothered to ask the Indians, who had long before inhabited America, if they had a problem with relinquishing the land they had previously lived freely upon. The French, however, were far more interested in trapping beavers and such, than devouring the land for their own personal use; they also integrated themselves into the Indian culture, and agreed to share the land with them. It is for this reason that most of the Indians in the East decided to join forces with the French. Perhaps they accepted what they perceived as the lesser evil, but who knows. In the end, however, the victory would be for the English, at least for this war. There would be many other smaller battles won by the Indians.

At the closing of the war, England was in bad shape economically. It had spent every penny on the war in America, and was desperate for funds. It decided that its colonists should pay it back for all of its support, and that the most effective way for them to do so would be to increase taxes, and tighten the trade laws. The colonists, however, were not as keen about the idea. In fact, they were furious. They called the first Continental Congress into action, and decided to ignore England's financial demands. They said no.

Problems began. Anti-English sentiments were on the rise. First came the Boston Massacre of 1770. Five English colonists were shot dead in front of the tax collection office by English redcoats (soldiers) because snowballs were thrown at them. Then came the Boston Tea Party, an incident in which groups of colonists boarded English tea ships in the Boston harbor and dumped hundreds of boxes of tea into the ocean as a protest against England's tax laws. Then came "Common Sense," a pamphlet written by Thomas Paine, an English writer who had settled in America shortly before the American Revolution. The pamphlet was intended to persuade the colonists that a complete separation from England was necessary if democracy and independence were going to be realized. It wasn't long before war was once again imminent, only this time the colonists were fighting against their mother England. The American Revolution broke out.

During the war, Congress decided that a formal document needed to be written in order to properly declare independence from England. The members chose Thomas Jefferson, our second founding father, to compose such a document—they called it the *Declaration of Independence*. Several other founders such as Benjamin Franklin, John Adams, John Hancock, and George Washington contributed to the final draft. It was signed and officially enacted on July 4, 1776. The significance it bears is outstanding.

First of all, it stated *why* the colonies were breaking their connections to England—they wanted to be self-governed, and they wanted equal rights among individuals. Second, it stated *what* England's injustices had been—there was a lack of law and order, they had been deprived trials by jury, they had been forced to pay taxes unjustly, and England had interrupted their trade. Last, it *declared* America as an independent nation, with no ties whatsoever to England.

Shortly after the drafting of the *Declaration of Independence,* Congress wrote the *Articles of Confederation*. The articles represented the first outline for American government. It established a union of equal states, known as the Confederation. Since the people were still wary of any government at all, little power was actually given to the Confederation. As a result, not a whole lot was accomplished. First of all, each state had its own currency. There was no national court to protect people's rights, there was no means of enforcing the law, it couldn't levy taxes, and there was no head of state or president. Congress soon realized that this was somewhat silly, and in an effort to improve upon what it had already written, Congress called a second meeting into action. This would change America forever.

What began as an elaboration of the *Articles of Confederation,* actually culminated in the writing of a whole new constitution. This constitution was different, because it explained not only the need for a central government, but the ideas and powers delegated to that government as well. The founders wanted to make it perfectly clear what the government could and could not do.

The preamble of the *Constitution* is the table of contents, so to speak, and actually makes sense when read carefully. It goes like this:

> ***We the People of the United States, in order to form a more perfect Union, establish justice, insure domestic tranquillity, provide for the common defense, promote the general welfare, and secure the blessings of liberty to ourselves and our posterity, do ordain and establish this Constitution for the United States of America.***

In other words, the purpose of the *Constitution* is to: (1) improve upon the *Articles of Confederation*, (2) ensure justice, (3) maintain peace and order, (4) defend the nation against all enemies, (5) create a better life for all, and (6) protect our freedoms as American citizens.

Additionally, seven articles, or parts, were included as well. These specifically enumerated the powers delegated to the government. The first article provides us with a Congress, made up of two houses, the Senate and the House of Representatives, and details their duties for us—several of which are creating new laws, declaring war, and levying taxes. Specific qualifications to be a representative of the House of Representatives include having attained the age of twenty-five years, having had U.S. citizenship for at least seven years, and living within the state that elects him or her. Representatives are elected every two years, and may serve a two-year term. Specific qualifications for being a senator (a representative of the Senate) include having attained the age of thirty years, having had U.S. citizenship for at least nine years, and living within the state that elects him or her. Senators can serve six-year terms. The second article provides us with a president and a vice president, and an explanation of their powers. The president is the commander in chief of the armed forces and of the National Guard. He or she is also empowered to pardon people, and appoint government officials into office (such as members of the Supreme Court). The president is essentially responsible for ensuring that all laws of the land are enforced, and that the nation is secured from all foreign and domestic attack. In order to be president, one must be a native-born U.S. citizen, be at least thirty-five years old, and have lived in the U.S.

for at least fourteen years. The third article provides us with supreme, federal, and national courts. The fourth article explains how the federal and state governments will function together. The fifth article explains how changes and amendments may be made. Amendments to the Constitution are proposed by Congress (by a two-thirds vote by the Senate as well as the House), or by two-thirds of the states' legislatures. In addition, each amendment must be approved by three-fourths of the states in order to become part of the Constitution. The sixth article states that the *Constitution,* and treaties and laws passed by Congress are the highest laws of the land. It requires that all government officials promise to support the laws of the land. It also states that government officials cannot be denied a position based on their religious beliefs. The seventh article states that as soon as nine of the thirteen states ratify (approve) the *Constitution,* it would officially go into effect.

Finally, there is a section reserved for the Bill of Rights. The addition of the Bill of Rights to the *Constitution* is perhaps the most significant event in American government history, since it was the reason that opponents to the *Constitution* agreed to ratify the *Constitution* in the first place. Simply stated, when it was first proposed, there were many people who disagreed that there should be a central government at all (the anti-federalists); they believed that any government was bad. More importantly, there were no freedoms granted to the people; they believed that without a guarantee of specific rights to the people, there was simply no point to the *Constitution* at all. It is for this reason that some of the (federalist) members of Congress, notably, James Madison, promised that if the *Constitution* was ratified, a

Bill of Rights would be added. And that is what happened. By 1791 the *Constitution* had officially adopted the Bill of Rights.

Eventually, the *Constitution* grew to include twenty-seven amendments, most of which were included between the late 1700s and the 1900s. Though amendments eleven through twenty-seven are as equally an important part of the *Constitution* as the original Bill of Rights, they will be only briefly covered in the latter portion of this book as a reference point from which you can witness when, why, and how amendments were added as times and circumstances changed. As mentioned earlier, the *Constitution* continues to live—it will evolve and adapt to the people it serves to honor and protect.

The First Amendment

*Restriction of free thought and free speech
is the most dangerous of all subversions.
It is the one un-American act
that could most easily defeat us all.*

—JUSTICE WILLIAM O. DOUGLAS

WHAT IT IS

CONGRESS SHALL MAKE NO LAW RESPECTING AN ESTABLISHMENT of religion, or prohibiting the free exercise thereof; or abridging the freedom of speech, or of the press; or of the right of the people peaceably to assemble, and to petition the Government for a redress of grievances.

WHAT IT MEANS

The First Amendment is very simple—it promises everyone the right to free speech, the right to practice any religion they choose, and the right of the press to gather and distribute information. It also ensures that if someone doesn't like something, he or she can petition to have it changed. It means that people can say anything they want, believe in anything they want, associate (or disassociate) with anyone they would like, and participate in any activity they choose, so long as they do not infringe upon the equal rights of others. Individuals are, essentially, free to engage their minds and bodies in whatever way they choose, provided they do not interfere with another person who engages in these same liberties. For example, you as an individual are entitled to pray to your particular deity, but you cannot force another to build a church from which you can practice your religion. Similarly, you have the right to express your opinion, but you cannot force someone else to build a podium from which you can speak. There is a shared blanket of protection, and as soon as I pull your side of the blanket over me—that is, as soon as I have just declared my rights as superior to yours—I have just violated the First Amendment.

HOW IT IS MISUSED TODAY

One would think that the safest place to exercise one's First Amendment rights would be on college campuses, where the quest for truth and the exchange of ideas are student attractions. After all, it is here, in academia, where knowledge and information is often first conceived, and then filtered into the rest of the community. Society depends on these universities and colleges to provide it with accurate, well designed facts and ideas which citizens can apply to their own lives. Unfortunately, however, the increasing trend toward political correctness and tolerance among people on campus has not only intimidated students from voicing their opinions and concerns (and thus suppressed the circulation of ideas), but has actually reshaped the idea of what education is meant to accomplish. Sitting in the classroom, many are faced with the decision to either voice their opinion and prepare for potential ridicule from other students, or keep quiet, and remain safe and protected. The pressure to become tolerant and accepting of all people, cultures, behaviors, and ideas, so long as they fit the mold of what administrators believe will unify, rather than differentiate students, can be so overwhelming that many students have simply chosen silence. The stress is real, and students are afraid.

One study cited that over 70 percent of the nation's campuses have drafted or enforced speech codes (standards for acceptable speech). Such codes include the things students can and cannot say, and determine for the students the ways in which they may or may not express them. Students must curtail their opinions and ideas in school newspapers, in campus organizations, and in the classroom. They must, in essence, concern themselves with how others will react, rather than what they may have to say.

Though there have been attempts to create bills which would enable students to take legal action against schools that violate students' First Amendment right to free speech, many are still pending within judiciary committees and subcommittees. These bills, which would focus on empowering the students by giving them the right to sue their schools for imposing restrictive speech codes, might be one such step in eliminating the trend of what First Amendment advocates call a different kind of intolerance—an intolerance for the United States Constitution.

Most people would perhaps agree that intolerance in the form of hostility among individuals is not a positive thing. However, forcing people to be tolerant of one another by taking away their constitutional rights hardly appears to be a step in the right direction.

With regard to freedom of speech . . .

THE EXTREMES

1) People can say whatever they want, even if it incites action that results in the harm of others. In other words, a person can scream "fire!" in a closed auditorium, resulting in multiple injuries, and will not be held responsible. In this instance, the government has no right to limit speech under any circumstances.

2) People cannot say whatever they want, since it might offend or harm another person. In other words, a person might say something which hurts another's feelings or which causes that person to inflict harm upon him or herself. In this instance, the government should limit speech, and punish the individual who caused the wounded feelings.

WHAT MOST PEOPLE WOULD AGREE

In most situations, people can say whatever they want. The only exceptions are when people may be potentially harmed in some physical way, or, in an effort to fight discrimination, when certain groups of people are harassed or treated unfairly based on their ethnicity, culture, gender, etc. For example, one cannot yell "fire!" in a movie theater for the simple reason that people could get hurt, nor can one refuse employment to someone based on the above differences. The government should limit speech, then, if it reveals itself in the form of verbal or physical harassment.

BONES OF CONTENTION

1) It is the government's responsibility to protect citizens from offensive speech. The government needs to monitor what people around the nation are saying, so as to ensure that no one says anything damaging about, for example, the major institutions within current society. In order to keep the United States a strong, unified nation, there must be an effort made to keep unpatriotic comments quieted. This is done for the good of society.

2) It is never the government's responsibility to protect citizens from any kind of speech, especially when it is enforced for the purpose of some patriotic, social good. People have the right, as American citizens, to say whatever they would like, especially when it comes to challenging the established institutions, and voicing individual opinions and philosophies in an effort to create change for the good of everyone.

The Second Amendment

The principal foundations of all states are good laws and good arms; and there cannot be good laws where there are not good arms.

—NICCOLÒ MACHIAVELLI

WHAT IT IS

A WELL REGULATED MILITIA, BEING NECESSARY TO THE security of a free State, the right of the people to keep and bear arms, shall not be infringed.

WHAT IT MEANS

The Second Amendment is perhaps the most important amendment. First of all, it entitles the American people to an army, navy, and marines for their protection against all foreign attack. That is, it ensures that there will always be a militia to protect their freedoms and their rights. Secondly, it promises the right of every American citizen to own and use guns. The right of individuals to personally own guns is especially important, since no one can ever be certain that the government will always be able to protect individual rights; there is always the possibility that the American government could be overthrown by a more powerful foreign nation, thereby rendering all liberties and freedoms obsolete. Furthermore, American citizens can never be guaranteed that their own government will always serve their best interests. The founders understood the tyrannical nature of government, and so empowered the people by giving them the right to own guns as a means of protecting themselves from their own government. They wanted to send a very clear message to the government that the people—not the government—were in charge. They believed that the right to own guns was necessary to protect all individual rights. Thus, as perceived in this light, the Second Amendment secures the Bill of Rights. The Bill of Rights without the Second Amendment is much like a turtle without its shell—vulnerable. Without it, there's no protection. There is no guarantee. There is no freedom.

HOW IT IS MISUSED TODAY

The right to keep and bear arms is perhaps the most controversial of all the amendments given the national attention and current antigun sentiments it has received over the past several years. The debate between Second Amendment advocates and those who believe it to be nothing more than an antiquated right continues. The recent passing of the Brady Bill, which requires a mandatory seven-day waiting period for the purchase of a handgun, is one such example of the latter's success in undermining the Constitution. The ways in which the government in this instance (and in most every other instance) has disempowered the people are very subtle, and often quite convincing. Keeping this in mind, it is not surprising that the Brady Bill was passed into law.

The Brady Bill was initially proposed during the Reagan administration, after Jim Brady, then White House press secretary, was shot and disabled in John Hinckley's attempted assassination of President Reagan. Naturally, there was a tremendous amount of concern that this sort of thing would happen again, and that this was, in fact, happening all around the nation every day. Brady Bill supporters believed that passing a federal law which would require individuals to wait (at least) seven days for the purchase of a handgun would make it that much more difficult for people like John Hinckley to harm or kill someone. These supporters argued that they were not encroaching on individuals' constitutional rights, since they weren't taking away people's Second Amendment right to own guns, but rather delaying a process which would not even affect most law-abiding citizens anyway. In fact, they argued, it would rather ensure that law-abiding citizens were *that much more* protected. In other words, the passing of the Brady Bill would not affect law-abiding citizens, since they would not be purchasing a handgun for the purpose of harming someone. Criminals, on the other hand, would be affected, since it would give the federal government ample time to check their criminal records, and locate any other valuable information that might disallow them from buying a handgun and harming someone. Though there were other arguments which supported the Brady Bill—such as decreasing the suicide rate, and keeping otherwise law-abiding citizens from doing anything stupid in the heat of the moment—none was quite as compelling as the one which deters criminals from carrying out violent acts against others. The ensuing question, then, is who is going to be there to protect law-abiding citizens from the criminals who have already purchased their guns off the street?

It is important to keep in mind that while the Brady Bill is an ostensibly reasonable way to control violence and crime (though this has been both refuted and supported by studies time and time again), it is still a violation of an individual's constitutional rights. However subtle and insignificant the Brady Bill might be in the eyes of many people today, the vision of *what could be* in the future is blinding. The Brady Bill is just another step in a slow, subtle process which just might eventually leave the American people without their protective turtle shells. We must not forget the fates of the Cambodians, the Bosnians, and those who fought against the injustices at Tienanmen Square. These people were killed and tortured for fighting for the very freedoms that many people in this country now take for granted.

The controversy surrounding the Second Amendment reminds me of the time I was mugged by a man with a gun. It was just around the time the Brady Bill was passed, and as he stood behind me with his gun jabbing me in the center of my back, I couldn't help but for an instant wonder if he, like myself, had to wait the seven-day waiting period to protect himself.

With regard to gun control . . .
THE EXTREMES

1) Everyone has the right to own any weapon they choose, including handguns, bazookas, and nuclear bombs. There should be no restrictions whatsoever, and the government should not be able to pass laws which would impose on individuals' rights to distribute, purchase, and own guns.

2) No one has the right to own any kind of gun, whether it is to be used for protection or for recreation. The only people who can own and operate a gun are members of the police and the military. The government should impose maximum restrictions on the distribution, purchase, and ownership of guns, and prosecute to the fullest extent anyone who violates the law.

WHAT MOST PEOPLE WOULD AGREE

U.S. citizens have the right to own handguns for protection, as well as for recreation. The distribution and sale of guns should, however, be regulated. In other words, the government should require citizens to have their guns registered by and licensed within the state in which they live. This way, the government can better control the way guns are used.

BONES OF CONTENTION

1) Everyone has the right to own and operate most any gun they choose. The government should not be permitted to force individuals to register their guns, nor should it be able to require them to attain a license, since both are attempts at restricting the individual's constitutional right to own guns.

2) No one automatically has the right to own guns. They must, for example, prove to their government that they deserve to operate a gun. Individuals should only be allowed to rent and use guns in designated areas and places of business, where their use can be regulated.

The Third Amendment

This provision speaks for itself . . . that a man's house shall be his own castle, privileged against all civil and military intrusion.

—JUSTICE JOSEPH STORY

WHAT IT IS

No soldier shall, in time of peace be quartered in any house, without the consent of the owner, nor in time of war, but in a manner to be prescribed by law.

WHAT IT MEANS

This amendment protects you from being forced to house a soldier during times of peace. During wartime, however, Congress may pass a law requiring individuals to house soldiers, if needed.

HOW IT IS MISUSED TODAY

This is perhaps the only amendment which has not been abused in recent times. During the Civil War, however, people's bodies, homes, and personal property were confiscated repeatedly, so that the feuding northern and southern governments could more effectively harm one another. If the government wanted to station a camp on an individual's property because it could be utilized, then they did so. The states became police regulated, whereby the individual did not feel protected from having their home and private property invaded. The government forced people to allow soldiers to stay in their homes, take their private property, and demand their services. This is not to say that there were many individuals who did not offer their services and private property, since many patrons of the war were volunteers. However, there were many similar interests involved among the people and their armies. Perhaps the lesson learned from this war is responsible for having since protected us.

With regard to housing soldiers . . .

THE EXTREMES

1) At any time, the government should be able to force people to house soldiers. It is everyone's obligation and in everyone's best interest to contribute to their country. The government should incarcerate those who do not comply.

2) Never, under any circumstances, even when the entire country's population depends upon it, can the government force people to house soldiers. No one has an obligation to their country.

WHAT MOST PEOPLE WOULD AGREE

The government cannot force people to house soldiers. Instead, the people should help by encouraging one another to contribute in some way during a time of national crisis.

BONES OF CONTENTION

1) The government should encourage people to house soldiers since it is a positive contribution to our country. The government should reward those who comply, but not punish those who do not. For example, it should give those who help out a tax break.

2) The government can never force people to house soldiers; it is unconstitutional and cannot be justified even if it is democratically voted into law, since there will always be people who are forced to do something they do not want to do.

The Fourth Amendment

*They that can give up essential liberty
to obtain a little temporary safety
deserve neither liberty nor safety.*

—BENJAMIN FRANKLIN

WHAT IT IS

THE RIGHT OF THE PEOPLE TO BE SECURE IN THEIR PERSONS, houses, papers, and effects, against unreasonable searches and seizures, shall not be violated, and no warrants shall issue, but upon probable cause, supported by oath or affirmation, and particularly describing the place to be searched, and the persons or things to be seized.

WHAT IT MEANS

It is unconstitutional for anyone, including the federal government and its agencies, to search and/or seize an individual's body or private property, unless a specific, court-approved search warrant is presented. It means that people have the right to keep their lives and property (which are really one and the same) private, unless there is probable cause that a crime has been committed. If, for example, there is probable cause that someone is bashing in car windows with a baseball bat, then the police (the government) can go to that person's home with a search warrant and seize the bat.

There is no such thing as a *general* search warrant, or a *general* search and seizure of one's private property. A government agency, whether it be the police, the Federal Bureau of Investigation (FBI), the Drug Enforcement Agency (DEA), or the Bureau of Alcohol, Tobacco, and Firearms (BATF), cannot simply show up at one's home and demand to search it for "evidence." It must, for example, specify that it is looking for the bat. Furthermore, any evidence that is found which was not originally specified in the warrant cannot be used as evidence in court. If it finds an unregistered (illegal) gun in the person's home while searching for the bat, it may seize but not use the gun as incriminating evidence in court. The gun is inadmissible since it was unconstitutionally seized.

HOW IT IS MISUSED TODAY

The O. J. Simpson case is perhaps the most widely publicized criminal case of recent times. It is responsible for teaching millions of American people the law of the land, the justice system, and the Constitution. In the preliminary hearing, the defense argued that evidence found on Simpson's property was illegally searched and seized, since a legal search warrant was not presented before the police entered his property. The prosecution, however, claimed that the police entered his property in "good faith" (with the intent to help, rather than harm), since it had sufficient reason to believe that a crime was in action or that someone was injured. The police department's course of action was therefore justified (based on a Supreme Court decision which upheld this "good faith" clause) with probable cause and good intention. Though the debate is a tricky one, loaded with points of contention, the fact of the matter is that Simpson's constitutional right to privacy under the Fourth Amendment was not strictly honored, regardless of his guilt or innocence. This happens all the time.

With regard to search and seizure . . .

THE EXTREMES

1) The government can search and seize private property without a search warrant whenever it wants. It may use its own judgment when confiscating people's private property, and should not be held accountable for the mistakes it makes, since it is always looking out for the people's best interests.

2) Under no circumstances can the government search and seize someone's private property, even if it believes that lives are endangered. It must always have the consent of the owner of the property, or it is to be held liable for its illegal actions, and punished to the full extent of the law.

WHAT MOST PEOPLE WOULD AGREE

The government cannot search and seize someone's private property without a legal search warrant, unless there is strong probable cause that a crime is being committed or that someone's life is endangered. The government (and its agencies) should be held accountable for its actions if it abuses this amendment.

BONES OF CONTENTION

1) The government should be allowed to search and seize someone's private property if it does so in good faith; give the government more control to decide at its own discretion which circumstances do and do not require a search warrant. In other words, have faith in the government to always use its good judgment.

2) The government should always be treated with skepticism; the only time a search warrant is not necessary is when someone's life is threatened. Government agencies should be audited on a regular basis so that an account of its actions is always under strict scrutiny.

The Fifth Amendment

*The authority of government . . .
can have no pure right over my person and property
but what I concede to it.*

—H. D. THOREAU

WHAT IT IS

No person shall be held to answer for a capital, or otherwise infamous crime, unless on a presentment or indictment of a Grand Jury, except in cases arising in the land or naval forces, or in the militia, when in actual service in time of war or public danger; nor shall any person be subject for the same offense to be twice put in jeopardy of life or limb; nor shall be compelled in any criminal case to be witness against himself, nor be deprived of life, liberty, or property, without due process of law; nor shall private property be taken for public use, without just compensation.

WHAT IT MEANS

First of all, individuals cannot be tried for a crime unless a grand jury has filed an indictment against them; that is, a grand jury believes that there is enough evidence against that individual to formally accuse them of committing the crime. It does not mean that they are guilty; it means that they are a suspect. The only exception to this is when a person is in the military, and special circumstances, such as national security, obviate the indictment process.

Once an indictment has been filed against an individual, a court date is set, and he or she is obligated under the law to attend. Though an individual cannot be forced to testify against him or herself, he or she may choose to do so on their own behalf. This protects the individual from self-incrimination, but it may also aid him or her in their defense; the individual's lawyer will usually advise him or her on this decision.

The verdict of a criminal trial is final, and a person cannot be tried twice for the same crime. If the jury cannot agree on a verdict, or a mistrial has been granted because the individual's rights have been violated, then a new trial is set.

Finally, the individual is never to be deprived of life, liberty, or property without "due process of law." Individuals are to be safe and secure in the privacy of their own home, and the government cannot confiscate one's property without just compensation. In other words, the government cannot take away one's property and home just because he or she has been convicted of a crime. If the government believes that the person's property is somehow valuable to the public—that is, in the best interests of the community—then it must compensate by offering an equal exchange.

HOW IT IS MISUSED TODAY

Most people are taught to respect the private property of others at a very young age. In fact, it is during childhood when some of the oldest adages concerning private property are initially introduced: "Don't take what doesn't belong to you," "Ask permission first," "Put it back where you got it," and "What do you say?" From these common courtesies grew agreements, boundaries, and contracts between people which outlined the way people would use, sell, and protect their private property.

People view their property as extensions of themselves. It is for this reason that the final clause to the Fifth Amendment was added to the Constitution—to serve as a reminder that to value an individual is to value that person's private property. Furthermore, to say that the government cannot take away someone's property without "just compensation" is to say that the two cannot be separated. They are supposed to be equally protected. Additionally, the due process clause of the amendment—which is basically intended to limit government power by requiring government officials to abide by certain procedures of conduct—requires the government to deal with property issues in a similarly just manner. Just compensation, therefore, compels the government to not only justify when they confiscate someone's property, but pay for it as well. More importantly, it limits the degree to which it can regulate and restrict property ownership without actually paying the cost of it. In other words, if the government is going to create a law or a mandate which requires an individual to do something to his or her property, then it must, at the very least, pay for it.

Today, however, such obligations on owners by the government continue to grow. There are laws, created every day, which unjustly force private owners to abide by the government's demands. Millions of people purchase property, expecting to build upon it, cultivate it, and otherwise use it for their own business, and then realize that the government has placed certain restrictions upon their property. In some areas, for example, people cannot extirpate a tree that is eroding their driveway because the area they live in is protected under a "you can't even cut down your own tree" mandate. Similarly, thousands of homes have burned to the ground because the government has forbidden owners from clearing away dry, hazardous brush from around their homes. Others, such as farmers and individuals living in newly developed areas, cannot set rodent traps on their property, even though such rodents are destroying their crops and infesting their homes.

The list of restrictions goes on. Private owners are having a difficult time challenging such strictly enforced mandates, having little financial backing after their initial investments. These owners are thus not only paying the full cost of owning their property (initial purchase, development, labor, and upkeep), but also paying the price of mandates which either impose an obligation on them to do something, or require them to pay for damages which result from such mandating in the first place. As a result, there is often little incentive for the average person to take the risk of attaining the American dream of private property ownership.

With regard to just compensation . . .

THE EXTREMES

1) The government can take away private property whenever it wants. It needn't make justifications for confiscating people's property, since it is its job to provide for the social good. Restrictions and mandates are therefore good, since they benefit a greater societal need.

2) The government can never take away someone's private property. Confiscating an individual's property, under any circumstances, is theft, not to mention unconstitutional. Restrictions and mandates are nothing more than an insidious way for the government to take away individual rights.

WHAT MOST PEOPLE WOULD AGREE

The government must justify itself when taking away an individual's private property. The only time it should place restrictions on private property is when there is compelling evidence that such property is beneficial or potentially harmful to the public. In this case, the individual should be given equal or greater compensation. Many mandates today are unfair and should be challenged.

BONES OF CONTENTION

1) Most of the time, the government can justify taking away someone's property—this is especially true in cases where individuals' rights have been taken away.

The government doesn't have to compensate criminals for their property, for example, since criminals have no rights.

2) Most of the time, the government cannot justify taking away someone's property. Even criminals, who have relinquished some of their rights, are protected under the Constitution. The only time the government can place restrictions on or confiscate someone's property is if the property is somehow endangering the lives and/or property of others.

The Sixth Amendment

*The jury system puts a ban
upon intelligence and honesty, and a premium
upon ignorance, stupidity and perjury.*
—MARK TWAIN

WHAT IT IS

IN ALL CRIMINAL PROSECUTIONS, THE ACCUSED SHALL ENJOY THE right to a speedy and public trial, by an impartial jury of the State and district wherein the crime shall have been committed, which district shall have been previously ascertained by law, and to be informed of the nature and cause of the accusation; to be confronted with the witnesses against him; to have compulsory process for obtaining witnesses in his favor, and to have the assistance of counsel for his defense.

WHAT IT MEANS

Once individuals have been formally accused of a crime, and they fully understand why they have been so accused, they have the right to several freedoms.

First of all, a speedy trial protects them from being forced to serve time in jail for a crime that they may not have committed—they are, after all, innocent until proven otherwise. It also minimizes pretrial stress, which may impair them to adequately defend themselves.

Second, individuals have the right to a public trial so that their constitutional rights are protected throughout the criminal process; the viewing public ensures that their rights are upheld and that they are treated justly. It ensures the integrity of the testimonies, and ultimately helps the public keep an eye on the judicial system.

Third, individuals are entitled to an open-minded, unbiased jury, whereby all of the evidence is considered objectively. The jury selection process is designed to filter out those individuals who might otherwise pose a threat to their rights. An individual wouldn't want a potential juror who despises people with facial hair to convict him or her of a crime simply because he or she has a mustache.

Fourth, a criminal trial must be held in the state and/or district wherein the crime was committed, for the simple reason that different states and/or districts have different laws. It would be unjust, for example, for a man to be charged with illegal gambling in California, even though he actually engaged in this behavior in Nevada, where gambling is legal.

Fifth, people have the right to have witnesses testify both for and against them. This clause was added since criminals in England did not have the right to obtain witnesses in their defense.

Finally, individuals have the right to an attorney at the public's expense.

HOW IT IS MISUSED TODAY

The Sixth Amendment has suffered most, not necessarily because people are deliberately ignoring it, but because there are so many obstacles with which it must contend. The creation of new laws and new crimes have enabled legislators to get away with both delaying the criminal process and overlooking the rights of the accused. Individuals charged with crimes are waiting years before their case goes to trial, and with so many "criminals" impacting the system, many of whom are waiting in jail, there is an increasing tendency to delay the trial. This is, of course, not surprising since the system has to contend with so many other criminal cases.

One of the more recent controversies surrounding Sixth Amendment protection has to do with the right of the accused to be confronted by the accuser and witnesses against him or her. On the one hand, some argue that there are situations in which there exists a greater responsibility to protect the accuser and adverse witnesses than it is to protect the accused; victims of physical, sexual, and mental abuse are often too frightened or otherwise incapacitated to confront their abuser, and are thus exempt from their constitutional duty. Strict adherents to the Sixth Amendment, however, believe the opposite—that the accused has the right to confront the accuser and/or witness through cross-examination. Since it is the accuser—the prosecution—that bears the burden of proof, it is therefore necessary and obligatory that the accuser stand witness against the person he or she has so accused. Furthermore, the absence of the accuser and/or witness based upon some arbitrary scale of vulnerability is likely to instill bias in an otherwise unbiased jury. The act of the accuser not testifying against the accused could perhaps be reason itself for the jury (and the public for that matter) to render a not guilty verdict.

With regard to a speedy trial and confronting the accused . . .

THE EXTREMES

1) Individuals charged with a crime have no rights—once that person enters the criminal justice system, they must wait their turn to go to trial. No individual should expect to have a speedy trial, since it is his or her own fault for breaking the law. Furthermore, the accused doesn't have the right to force his or her accuser to confront him or her, since the accused doesn't have any rights.

2) Even an individual charged with a serious crime has rights—just because that person has entered the system does not mean that he or she must wait for a trial. All individuals have the right to a speedy trial, regardless of how impacted the system might be. Furthermore, the accused has the right to be confronted by his or her accuser, regardless of its effect on the accuser.

WHAT MOST PEOPLE WOULD AGREE

Everyone has the right to a speedy trial; no one should be forced to wait an inordinate amount of time for their trial. It is unfair that some individuals receive speedy trials, while others are forced to wait in jail for months or years. In most cases, when the accuser is capable of testifying against the accused, he or she should bear the responsibility of confrontation. Only in instances of severe abuse, as in the case of sexually abused children or victims of explicit violence, should the accuser waive their obligation.

BONES OF CONTENTION

1) Individuals charged with a crime have fewer rights than law-abiding citizens. That is, once a person has been charged with a crime, he or she has automatically forsaken most of their rights. Those individuals charged with lesser crimes will enter the system more speedily than those charged with more serious crimes. If the accuser doesn't want to confront the accused, then he or she doesn't have to. After all, the accuser has more rights than the accused.

2) All individuals have rights all of the time, regardless of the crime with which they have been charged. The justice system does provide a service to the people, but the people pay for it. It is the constitutional right of every American citizen to have a speedy trial, and the American justice system is obligated to the people—it works for the people. Similarly, the accuser has a constitutional obligation to confront the accused, since both are protected equally under law.

The Seventh Amendment

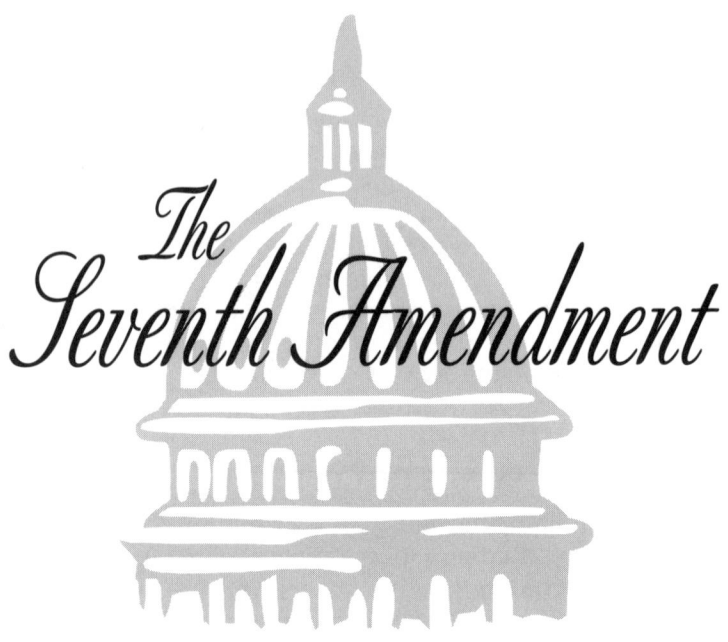

*We enact many laws that manufacture criminals,
and then a few that punish them.*

—Benjamin Tucker

WHAT IT IS

In suits at common law, where the value in controversy shall exceed twenty dollars, the right of trial by jury shall be preserved, and no fact tried by a jury, shall be otherwise reexamined in any Court of the United States, than according to the rules of the common law.

WHAT IT MEANS

*Y*ou are guaranteed a jury trial if the damage in question exceeds twenty dollars. Anything less is handled outside of court. If, for example, you steal something that amounts to a value of less than twenty dollars, then not much can be done to prosecute you in a court of law. A judge might keep the theft on file for the record, and may require that you return the stolen merchandise. If you're lucky, the other party will not even contact the police, but merely prohibit you from, for example, returning to their place of business.

HOW IT IS MISUSED TODAY

*T*here is not enough evidence to suggest that this amendment is abused today. Over two hundred years ago, when the Constitution was written, twenty bucks might have enabled you to buy a top-of-the-line horse. Today, although the majority of goods stolen probably ranges under the twenty dollar amount, the cost of prosecuting someone would not be a cost-efficient endeavor, to say the least. Today, one could probably buy a horse in lieu of trying the case. Essentially, if someone decided to steal a candy bar at a grocery store one evening and was caught in the process, he or she shouldn't expect any severe punishment. Chances are, people can steal their candy and eat it too.

With regard to damages which exceed twenty dollars . . .

THE EXTREMES

1) An individual is either guilty or innocent; either way, if the amount exceeds twenty dollars, the person is entitled to a trial by jury.

2) An individual is either innocent or guilty, though twenty dollars is never a sufficient amount of money to warrant a trial.

WHAT MOST PEOPLE WOULD AGREE

The nature of the accusation should determine whether a person should receive a jury trial; if the amount in question is a mere twenty-one dollars, then a judge should determine the person's guilt, and punish them accordingly. A jury trial is too expensive and time-consuming to be wasted on such a small offense.

BONES OF CONTENTION

1) Anyone who is accused of damages should receive a jury trial, regardless of the cost of those damages. If a person, for example, steals a candy bar from a grocery store, the owner of that grocery store has the right to bring that individual to court.

2) No one has the right to a jury trial just because the cost of damages exceeds twenty dollars. The judge should decide whether or not the individual accused of the crime should pay for the cost of damages.

The Eighth Amendment

*The punishment of the criminal is measured
by the degree of astonishment of the judge
who finds his crime incomprehensible.*

—F. W. NIETZSCHE

WHAT IT IS

Excessive bail shall not be required, nor excessive fines imposed, nor cruel and unusual punishments inflicted.

WHAT IT MEANS

This amendment states that courts of law must be fair when assessing bail and charging individuals with a particular crime. In other words, the punishment should fit the crime. An individual convicted of jaywalking, for example, should not serve hard time in the state penitentiary, just as the individual found guilty of first-degree murder should not be granted a reprieve and sent home on work parole. A person convicted of a victimless crime, that is, a person who harmed only him or herself, should not be given the same punishment as a person who has inflicted harm against another individual.

Posting bail supports the assumption of innocence—a presumably innocent person does not belong in jail. Strictly speaking, bail is the defendant's right to freedom during the pretrial interim. The amount of bail depends upon the crime with which the individual has been charged, the amount of evidence against the individual, previous convictions, family and community status, employment, and personal character. The type of bail can be money, property, or any other asset(s) the individual can use as assurance that he or she will be present at the trial.

HOW IT IS MISUSED TODAY

Today, there are people serving life sentences for growing marijuana. There are also individuals who are facing their third and fourth prison sentences for armed robbery and murder. Cruel? Unusual? Some think so.

When judges hand down sentences to convicted criminals, they are bound by law to follow certain state statutes. Every crime has its respective punishment, and the presiding judge often has little discretion when delivering a sentence.

There are two types of prison sentences—mandatory and nonmandatory. Mandatory sentences are those which must be served in their entirety, with no room for parole or a suspended sentence until the completion of the prison term. Judges have very little, if any, authority to override or change a mandatory sentence which has been already ascertained by state law. The nonmandatory sentence is one which may be interrupted for some compelling reason—the judge may use his or her discretion when assessing whether the individual's sentence should be prolonged or shortened. The judge will consider the individual's behavior once incarcerated, his or her family situation, previous record, or any other compelling reason which may persuade the judge to sentence more lightly or severely. Many judges do not like mandatory sentences for the stated reason that it allows them so little discretion. Hence, more often than not, it is the state, not the judge, passing judgment down upon the criminal. This is when sentencing may get cruel and unusual.

Prisons are overcrowded because there is no space. Why is there no space? Is it because there are too many criminals or too many crimes? Is it because there are too many mandatory sentences handed down? Many people are saying yes.

The scenario goes something like this: An individual serving a mandatory prison sentence (regardless of the crime) may not be released. They are therefore not only occupying a space, but preventing another criminal from entering the prison system. However, the (new) inmate must enter—he or she has committed a crime, and deserves to be in prison. The prison then has a dilemma:

Does it accept this new criminal and make the living situation for all inmates even more cramped and inhumane (perhaps cruel), or does it relieve itself of space, and allow someone else to go? More often than not, it makes a switch. It trades the new inmate for an old one serving a nonmandatory sentence. Dilemma solved, though temporarily. Chances are, the old inmate will return shortly to relieve someone else of his or her sentence. Like a train going around and around a track, the criminal almost inevitably ends up at the same destination.

Many people today are feeling the effects of this circulating criminal system. Repeat violent offenders keep coming back into society, robbing, molesting, disabling, and murdering citizens. Society is asking why. Why are these criminals released back into the streets clearly before they are ready? Why are these violent offenders being given nonmandatory sentences? Where is the justice?

There is no easy answer, of course. Perhaps we are asking the wrong questions. Maybe the question is not why there are so many criminals in the streets, but why there are so many crimes. Most people would agree that violent offenses deserve harsh punishments—the longer, mandatory punishments. But what about the nonviolent crimes—prostitution, drug use, gambling, burning money, failing to register a family pet, and other consensual crimes—which leave no victim behind? More importantly, why are the people convicted of these so-called "victimless" crimes receiving mandatory sentences?

Some people believe that it doesn't matter, that all crimes deserve punishment—even the consensual crimes, which they may believe are immoral or deserving of criminal status. However, this hardly seems appropriate when there are convicted rapists and murderers relinquishing their beds in prison to marijuana farmers. This does not seem fair. In fact, some believe it is cruel and unusual.

According to the National Center for Policy Analysis, "Only 17 percent of all murders lead to a prison sentence; only 5 percent of all rapes lead to a prison sentence; and a convicted felon goes to prison less than 3 percent of the time in cases of robbery, assault, burglary, and auto theft." In the book, *Ain't Nobody's Business If You Do,* Peter McWilliams cites a case in point. In Michigan, Alger County Circuit Court judge Charles Stark sentenced convicted rapist David Caballero to pay $975 for court fees, $200 for victim compensation, and serve a three-year probation; the conviction would then be erased forever off his record. Stark believed that Caballero was undeserving of a harsher sentence, since he was not only a young (twenty-one years old) criminal justice major student, but aspiring to be a police officer as well.

Regarding a young offender facing twenty years to life in prison without the possibility of parole for a first-time offense of possession of drugs estimated to be worth fifty dollars, the *Los Angeles Times* (April 25, 1993) stated, "Two more senior federal judges recently joined a growing list of their colleagues nationwide in refusing to preside over drug cases as a protest to the extreme and counter-productive sentences they are required to impose in these cases. We are sympathetic with their distress. Tough, inflexible federal sentencing rules, once considered 'the answer' to rising drug use and crime threaten to make a mockery of our federal criminal justice system." The same article quoted that "nearly 60 percent of all federal prisoners are now drug felons. Average prison terms for federal drug offenders have shot up 22 percent since 1986—while those of violent criminals fell by 30 percent."

The statistics are straightforward. They reflect a predicament which compromises the Eighth Amendment. Even judges who don't agree with state and federal laws which require them to hand down certain sentences would agree that certain criminals deserve harsher sentences—that they are to be held accountable for their actions, and must be punished to the full extent of the law. This seems just and fair. The judge can then assess each criminal case and deliver a fair sentence. What seems cruel and unusual is a system of government which consistently punishes nonviolent offenders in much the same way it does violent offenders.

Thus far, the message to the violent criminal population is for them to hope that there are far more nonviolent offenders serving time in their beds.

With regard to cruel and unusual punishment . . .

THE EXTREMES

1) Everyone convicted of a crime should be given the least severe punishment, regardless of the crime, since most people do not deserve the harsh punishment they are given. Most punishment is cruel and unusual, and should not be handed down as sentences.

2) Everyone convicted of a crime should be given the most severe punishment, regardless of the crime, since most people deserve the punishment they are given. A person convicted of growing marijuana should receive the same punishment as the individual convicted of murder, since breaking the law is breaking the law. Punishments handed down by the criminal justice system are not harsh enough.

WHAT MOST PEOPLE WOULD AGREE

Everyone convicted of a crime should be punished accordingly—the punishment should fit the crime. It is cruel and unusual to allow violent offenders back into society, when nonviolent offenders who are only a threat to themselves remain incarcerated. However, there are nonviolent offenses which still deserve to be punished.

BONES OF CONTENTION

1) Most laws are unjust and unconstitutional; thus, most punishments are too severe. Victimless crimes, such as prostitution, drug use, and gambling, should be legal, and thus not punishable by law. Violent crimes, such as armed robbery, murder, and rape, should be illegal, and thus punishable to the full extent of the law.

2) Most laws are just and constitutional; the government is too lenient, and allows immoral, violent people to roam the streets. We need harsher punishments to deter people from committing crimes.

The Ninth Amendment

*The only freedom which deserves the name
is that of pursuing our own good in our own way,
so long as we do not attempt to deprive others
of theirs, or to impede their efforts to obtain it.*

—John Stuart Mill

WHAT IT IS

The enumeration in the Constitution, of certain rights, shall not be construed to deny or disparage others retained by the people.

WHAT IT MEANS

This amendment is historically one of the most profound additions to the Constitution. Its purpose is to protect certain "retained" rights, even though they are not enumerated (written) in the Constitution. Retained rights include those naturally endowed to the people, otherwise known as "natural rights," and include the Bill of Rights as well as others not specified in the Constitution. Originally, those opposed to adding a Bill of Rights to the Constitution were concerned that people's freedoms would be limited to only those listed in the Bill of Rights. They believed that the government would inevitably take advantage of such an enumeration, since they could confine all freedoms to a list of ten. Operating within this rationale, retained rights would include the "leftovers"—those which remained *after* the federal government defined all of its powers. Any right which conflicted with a government interest or power was thus not a right retained by the people. This explanation contradicts the very essence of the Constitution, since it gives the federal government more freedom than it does the people. A more consistent explanation as it relates to the Constitution, then, would be that of a presumption of liberty, in which individuals are free to engage in any behavior they choose, provided that doing so does not violate another person's natural rights. Finally, according to John Locke, the very foundation for having a federal government is to ensure and protect all natural rights, including those both enumerated and unenumerated in the Constitution. The government must justify to the people any attempt—specifically, the creation of any new law— which might be interpreted as a violation (a disparaging) of this Ninth Amendment right.

HOW IT IS MISUSED TODAY

The Ninth Amendment has most often been applied to right to privacy issues, as have many of the other amendments, since it is very difficult to separate one's private property from one's own body, and what a person chooses to do with them. Some of the privacy issues today include people's personal associations—with other people, groups of people, organizations, ideas, and belief systems. Any intrusion of one's right to privacy is thus seen as a direct violation of the Ninth Amendment. Take, for example, mandatory drug tests.

In 1989 a seventh grade boy named James Acton refused a mandatory drug test for cocaine, amphetamines, and marijuana, which would have otherwise enabled him to play on the basketball team at his middle school in Oregon. Concerned that his constitutional rights had been violated, he, with the American Civil Liberties Union (ACLU), filed a lawsuit challenging the drug test. In 1994, a court of appeals in San Francisco agreed, ruling that such testing was a direct violation of Acton's right to privacy, especially since the school had no reason to believe that he was using drugs in the first place. Then, on June 26, 1995, the Supreme Court ruled (six to three) that random, routine drug testing of student athletes does not, in fact, pose a threat to their privacy rights, since there exists a greater responsibility to ensure the welfare and safety of the entire team. In fact, the *Los Angeles Times* (June 27, 1995) quoted Justice Scalia as saying, "There is an element of communal undress inherent in athletic participation."

The decision allows school officials to randomly test students of any grade regardless of any suspicion. The court ruled that the results of such testing could not be handed over to any state authority, and could only be used to suspend or terminate players from participating in their sport. Furthermore, players who tested positive could be required to undergo counseling.

The court's focus on student athletes is a peculiar one, since it not only singles out their privacy rights as somehow inferior to, for instance, the average nonparticipating student, but offers no consolation to those athletes who are drug free.

Why are the rights of a student any different from those of a student athlete? Why is it more important to keep athletes drug free? Is it because it is easier for the government to justify its actions? Is it because it knows that most parents would never tolerate such invasions? Is it perhaps, because the rights of a group (the team) are somehow superior to the rights of each individual team player? These are the kinds of questions people should be asking themselves, because such precedence is bound to be followed by similar courses of action.

American citizens are concerned about drugs, but should they become hardened to government actions which inevitably violate the personal bodies of their children? Most likely, this recent Supreme Court ruling will lessen the blow for similar actions to come.

Hopefully, the list of unenumerated rights will grow to include more privacy rights. As of today, however, there still seems to be a tremendous amount of discourse when it comes to the private lives of citizens.

With regard to unenumerated rights . . .

THE EXTREMES

1) People should decide for themselves what rights are protected under the Ninth Amendment. The government is never justified in making personal decisions for people, especially with regard to their privacy. Individuals are entitled to do whatever they choose with their own bodies—with whomever, however, whenever, and wherever.

2) People cannot decide for themselves what rights are protected under the Ninth Amendment. The government decides for the people what rights are and are not justified. Individuals do not have privacy; they cannot do whatever they choose.

WHAT MOST PEOPLE WOULD AGREE

The people decide what their rights are under the Ninth Amendment. They should be ascertained by the people, not the government, though there are circumstances in which the government may enact laws if it is done for the public good.

BONES OF CONTENTION

1) Individuals have the right to decide whatever they choose to do, as long as it does not infringe upon the equal rights of others. The Ninth Amendment should thus include any behavior which does not harm another individual. The people decide which rights are retained by the people and which are not.

2) Individuals do not have the right to do whatever they choose if it interferes with the powers assumed by the government. Thus, the Ninth Amendment reserves rights as it sees fit. The government chooses which rights are retained by the people, and which are not.

The Tenth Amendment

Each state is a sovereign, and thus may reclaim the grants which it has made to any agent whomsoever.

—JEFFERSON DAVIS

WHAT IT IS

THE POWERS NOT DELEGATED TO THE UNITED STATES BY THE Constitution, nor prohibited by it to the States, are reserved to the States respectively, or to the people.

WHAT IT MEANS

This amendment limits the power of the federal government by placing most of the responsibilities on the individual states. In other words, the states themselves control their own internal affairs. It is similar to the Ninth Amendment since it prohibits the federal government from taking away individual freedoms; if the federal government does not take away a particular freedom, then the people are entitled to that freedom. The federal government must specify what we cannot do, not what we can do. The state is supposed to help protect such freedoms. It determines, for example, which federal laws it will or will not enforce, and some states have more stringent laws than those of the federal government. Take for instance the Brady Bill discussed earlier in the chapter on the Second Amendment. The federal law requires a mandatory seven-day waiting period to purchase a handgun, yet the state of California chose to enforce a much stricter waiting period—two weeks.

Most of the time, it is in the state's best interest to enforce these "federal wishes" since the federal government has a tendency to make life a little tougher if it doesn't. A state which doesn't respect its federal government, for example, just might find itself with fewer highways, schools, and hospitals.

The responsibility of the state is much the same as that of a captain of a sports team. The federal government (the coach) relies on the state (the captain) to ascertain the rights of the team members as they relate to the Constitution (the rules of the game). As long as the rights of the individual player are honored by the captain, the game is fair. If this is not the case, and the captain should, for some reason, overlook the rights of the players as secondary to his or her own, then a new team captain can be elected. The only time the coach can interfere with the game is when the captain has unfairly benched the team or a team member for the game. It is important to remember that the same rules of the game apply (especially) to the coach.

HOW IT IS MISUSED TODAY

In order to understand what powers the federal government does not have, a brief discussion of the powers it does have is necessary. It has the right to collect taxes on the use, sale, and production of goods "uniformly," which means that the taxing should be imposed equally throughout the United States. It has the right to borrow money and regulate commerce with both foreign nations and among states. It has the right to coin and regulate the value of money. It has the right to punish those who commit crimes at sea. It has the right to establish post offices and roads. It has the right to declare war, to provide for and support the army, the navy, and the air force. It has the right—the obligation—to protect American citizens from foreign attack, as well as from violent offenses among one another. Finally, it has the right to create laws which are "necessary and proper for carrying into execution the foregoing powers, and all other powers vested by this Constitution in the government of the United States." It is this most generalized right of the government that has enabled it to create a multitude of laws over a multitude of matters which are not specifically enumerated in the Constitution. It has, according to many people, been the reason that the federal government has been able to infiltrate the lives of the American people with relative ease.

The only way to truly understand how the federal government has managed to violate the Tenth Amendment is to illuminate—without judgment—some of the laws it has created without the consent of the states, or more specifically, the people. Though there exist laws which some people agree or disagree with, it is important for each person to ask which powers the people will relinquish from themselves and entrust into the hands of the federal government. Since the government is obliged to protect the rights of all citizens, then any law imposed upon the people should be done so equally and uniformly, as stated in the Constitution. Today, many federal laws are never challenged because there exists a certain majority willing to support them. In other words, certain laws benefit some people—they are consistent with their philosophies and demands; while others disparage people—they are inconsistent with their philosophies and demands.

The recently repealed motorcycle helmet law, which required everyone riding a motorcycle to wear protective headgear, and which imposed a fine on anyone not wearing one, is one such example of a federal law which some deem unconstitutional. That is, they believe such mandating is outside the federal government's jurisdiction. The motorcycle helmet law, was, strictly speaking, a violation of the Tenth Amendment, since it imposed a federal obligation on states. States choosing to ignore the federal law risked losing highway funds.

Similar federal laws such as the 21 year old drinking age, the Clean Air Act, the Fair Labor Standards Act, the

Davis-Bacon Act, and the Americans with Disabillites Act, all carry the threat of the loss of funds if not enforced by the states. These federal laws have taken the power away from the states to decide for themselves what programs are in their own best interests, and at the same time, have brought some states to the brink of bankruptcy because the cost of compliance runs in the billions.

In any case, constitutionally speaking, the individual state should decide what laws are and are not applicable to the needs of their state, without any repercussions from the federal government.

With regard to who holds the power . . .

THE EXTREMES

1) Any power not granted to the people by the Constitution should be automatically given to the people; the people are empowered in much the same way as an obstinate child who argues, "You didn't say I couldn't!" to a scolding parent. The people, never the federal government, should decide what is in their best interest.

2) Any power not granted to the people in the Constitution is thus one that does not belong to them; the people are empowered only when the federal government says so. The federal government can thus create laws whenever it wants.

WHAT MOST PEOPLE WOULD AGREE

The federal government should butt out and let the people and their respective states decide what is best for them; there are too many restrictions and public mandates that interfere with private persons and their private business. The only time the federal government can create federal laws is when it is in the best interest of all people.

BONES OF CONTENTION

1) Any government intervention, except when it directly relates to the protection and welfare of the individual and country, is unacceptable. When in doubt, the power lies with the people. Individual states should govern as if they were independent nations, meeting the needs of their own citizens.

2) The federal government is boss; it should have the final word in all affairs, and veto states' decisions much like the president does for Congress' bills, especially since it is usually within its jurisdiction to do so. A strong federal government always has first priority in approving any law.

Amendments 11 through 27

This country, with its institutions, belongs to the people who inhabit it. Whenever they shall grow weary of the existing government, they can exercise their constitutional right of amending it, or their revolutionary right to dismember or overthrow it.

—Abraham Lincoln

THE FOUNDERS WERE WELL AWARE THAT TIMES AND circumstances would continue to change. They wanted to ensure a Constitution which would evolve with the changing needs of the country. James Madison wrote, "In framing a system which we wish to last the ages, we should not lose sight of the changes which ages will produce." Creating a system of government which would allow for the expansion of new amendments to the

Constitution was exactly the kind of flexibility the founders believed would enable the country to survive the ages.

So as to preserve the integrity of the Constitution, the founders needed to outline certain limitations (procedures) which the federal government would follow when amending the Constitution. They wanted to prevent shortsightedness and agendizing by the majority, and protect injustices against the minority. In other words, they wanted to make it difficult for government to ratify an amendment (keeping in mind that there have been over *148* amendments proposed since the beginning of today's 104th Congress, one of which—the flag burning amendment—may get ratified just before this book is published). To accomplish their goal, they created a system which would require the different levels of government to "check and balance" one another when proposing and ratifying new amendments. Two different methods were agreed upon.

The first way would necessitate that two-thirds of Congress—the Senate and the House of Representatives—would have to approve the proposed amendment. It then had to be ratified by either legislatures or national conventions in three-fourths of the states to become constitutional law.

The second (never really used) way would require the legislatures of two-thirds of the states to request an amendment from which Congress would then call for conventions to propose the amendment. It would become a law in the same way as the first procedure.

State legislatures and conventions are (constitutionally) permitted a seven-year time frame to ratify an amendment. Since the ratification of the Bill of Rights, there have been seventeen amendments to join the Constitution. They are as follows:

11TH AMENDMENT

Proposed on March 4, 1794, and ratified on February 7, 1795, the Eleventh Amendment was essentially a response to a Supreme Court decision in the case of *Chrisholm v. Georgia* (1793). It overturned the court ruling which supported the right of a South Carolina man to sue the state of Georgia over an inheritance. Proponents of this amendment didn't think it was fair that a citizen in one state sue another state in federal court—that is, they wanted state immunity against other states and foreign nations. Under this amendment, the only time a federal court can become involved is in areas of commerce, and when state officials are under scrutiny. This is especially true when an individual sues a state official for allegedly violating his or her constitutional rights.

12TH AMENDMENT

Proposed on December 9, 1803, and ratified on July 27, 1804, the Twelfth Amendment evolved out of the 1800 presidential election. At that time, each elector voted for two men, not specifying whom he wanted for president and whom he wanted for vice president. Whomever received the highest number of votes became president, and the runner-up became vice president. In 1800, Thomas Jefferson was running for the presidency and Aaron Burr was running for the vice presidency. However, in the final count it was discovered that both men had received the same number of votes. This cast the final decision into the hands of the House of Representatives, which appointed Thomas Jefferson. This amendment resolved this kind of dilemma from happening again, since it provided the electors with two ballots (rather than the traditional single ballot)—one for the presidency, and one for the vice presidency. Furthermore, it stated that if no person received the majority of votes for the presidency, then the House of Representatives would choose from the top three. Similarly, if no candidate received the majority of votes for the vice presidency, then the Senate would choose from the top two. The significance it bears is its contribution to party voting—the split ballot splits political parties!

13TH AMENDMENT

Proposed on January 31, 1865, and ratified on December 6, 1865, the Thirteenth Amendment represented a huge philosophical change in American history. For over a hundred years, the Constitution was a contradiction; it purported to ensure equality for all people—to secure their life, liberty, and pursuit of happiness—and yet all it actually accomplished was a good life for the white male citizen. There are numerous explanations from various historians as to the evolution of the Thirteenth Amendment. Most agree on the larger issues—the contributing political, social, and economic conditions—and reject the fallacy that slaves were freed out of a newfound respect for the human condition. Listed below are several of the factors which are generally agreed upon.

First of all, in 1863, during the Civil War, Abraham Lincoln abolished slavery in the Confederate states still in rebellion in his Emancipation Proclamation. By the end of the Civil War, most members of Congress were either Republicans or belonged to the Union, who, like Lincoln, espoused philosophies which were consistent with antislavery sentiments. Additionally, the war had apparently affected the way people perceived the allocation of powers between the federal and state governments. Their increasingly changing ideas favored a more powerful, united nation, one in which the federal government would assume a more heightened role in protecting the freedoms of its people—of all people. It was the first amendment to challenge states' rights and their ability to define the status of their own citizens.

14TH AMENDMENT

Proposed on June 13, 1866, and ratified on July 9, 1868, the Fourteenth Amendment finished what the Thirteenth Amendment started. Though slavery had been abolished after the Civil War, it did not prohibit the states from enacting laws, otherwise known as "black codes," which denied blacks many of their rights. In the South, blacks had very few, if any, property rights, voting rights, and many of the rights granted to American citizens in the Bill of Rights. They were permitted to do this since it was still constitutional—as far as the Constitution was concerned, only U.S. citizens were endowed with such rights. Since blacks were not citizens—in fact only counted as three-fifths of a person according to Article 1 of the Constitution— states were still able to legally deny them such rights. This amendment changed all of that. It granted all of the newly freed slaves full citizenship. Those Confederate states which didn't honor the amendment were threatened to be kept out of Congress and/or the Union. Similarly, any state which prohibited any adult male from voting would also have its representation in Congress reduced.

The Fourteenth Amendment also explained how people attained U.S. citizenship. It states that all people born in the United States, or are granted citizenship by law, are citizens. Anyone born in the U.S. by the parents of foreign diplomats or foreign enemies during wartime are not citizens, though children born outside of the United States by an American citizen are. Indians not paying taxes are not granted citizenship. Finally, this amendment was a promise to pay back the Union's debt, but not the Confederacy's, left over from the Civil War. Furthermore, former slave owners would not be compensated for their newly emancipated slaves.

15TH AMENDMENT

Proposed on February 26, 1869, and ratified on February 3, 1870, the Fifteenth Amendment was a response to a Republican political predicament. In 1868, Ulysses S. Grant, the Republican candidate for president, won 73 percent of the electoral vote and 52 percent of the popular vote. The general perception was that he won the presidency only because of the popular vote of Southern blacks, who had been granted the right to vote by Congress in many of the Southern states shortly after the Civil War. Though clearly in the lead in the electorate, some say Grant would have lost the presidency if it weren't for that very important sector's vote. The urgency to enfranchise the black voter was greater than ever.

First of all, the Democrats (the Confederates) were doing surprisingly well after the war. They were earning seats in Congress, and often neck and neck with the Republicans (the Union) in elections. Stories that Democrats were using scare tactics on the Southern black voter began to simmer. Eventually, in an attempt to counter the resurgent Democratic party, the Republicans decided that something needed to be done. They desperately needed the black vote if they were to remain in power, and so the Fourteenth Amendment was added to the Constitution. It protected the right of citizens to vote, regardless of "race, color, or [any other] previous condition of servitude."

16TH AMENDMENT

Proposed on July 12, 1909, and ratified on February 3, 1913, the Sixteenth Amendment overturned the 1895 Supreme Court ruling of *Pollack v. Farmers' Loan*, which had declared federal income tax laws unconstitutional. The amendment was proposed during the progressive era, a time of social, economic, and political change which called for an increase in government involvement. Advocates of the progressive movement wanted federal and state programs which would help people get back on their feet financially. There was an increasing trend toward economic disparity, a situation which some Americans found unfair; they wanted a redistribution of wealth and prosperity, and the Fourteenth Amendment was one such way that the government could achieve this goal. It was ratified, and from then on, Congress has continued to impose a federal tax on all sources of income.

17TH AMENDMENT

Proposed on May 13, 1912, and ratified April 8, 1913, the Seventeenth Amendment states that the Senate can no longer vote for its own members. It placed this power in the hands of U.S. citizens. This was perhaps one way that the people could more effectively "check and balance" the distribution of power.

18TH AMENDMENT

Proposed on December 18, 1917, and ratified on January 16, 1919, the Eighteenth Amendment was otherwise known as "national prohibition." It prohibited the use, sale, and transportation of alcoholic beverages. Some say that this amendment was the product of the temperance movement—of religious groups, churches, feminists, businessmen, teachers, and other political and social reformers who believed alcohol to be the degradation of American society. They succeeded, and the seventh largest industry in the nation had exactly one year to get it out of their system before national prohibition would go into effect. It would be the only amendment in U.S. history to be repealed.

19TH AMENDMENT

Proposed on June 4, 1919, and ratified on August 18, 1920, the Nineteenth Amendment gave women the right to vote in state and national elections. The result of much work by the feminist movement, it is also known as the "Anthony amendment," named after Susan B. Anthony, a woman whose contribution to women's rights earned her her own amendment.

20TH AMENDMENT

Proposed on March 2, 1932, and ratified on January 23, 1933, the Twentieth Amendment stated that the presidential term would begin on January 20 instead of March 4. It was passed to shorten the time between the election (November) and the time the president's term begins (January). This was implemented so as to remove the so-called "lame ducks"—presidents and legislators in Congress who were not reelected yet continued in office until the newly elected officials were inaugurated. This shortened the time they served in office by approximately four months.

21st AMENDMENT

Proposed on February 20, 1933, and ratified on December 5, 1933, this amendment repealed the Eighteenth Amendment, and empowered the individual states to decide the legality of alcohol sale and use. It was the only amendment to be repealed by the electorate rather than the legislators, and the only amendment to repeal another amendment.

During prohibition, there were many federal and state enforcement policies and laws—such as warrantless searches and seizures, laws which denied liquor for medicinal purposes, phone and wiretap surveillances, and increased fines and sentencing for convicted criminals—which accomplished little at the heart of the crusade against alcohol. Many people believed that prohibition encouraged crime; it increased the profit value of alcohol, drove its sale and production underground to the black market, introduced the Mafia's involvement, and increased violent offenses both within and outside the legal system. Since the stigma attached to those individuals who became alcohol abusers was so great, few actually sought help and reform, therefore discouraging rehabilitation and recovery. Legalizing alcohol, it was argued, would at least allow the government to tax its manufacture and sale, thereby creating jobs and programs for people in need of help.

Others believed prohibition to be nothing more than racial bias toward immigrants whose cultures embraced the religious and social aspects of alcohol use (noting that sacramental wine in the Catholic church was, for some superior reason, legal and socially acceptable throughout prohibition).

For different cultures, for religion, for law enforcement, for the judicial system, for medicine, for rehabilitation, and for individual rights, the use of alcohol was at issue. The increased disrespect for the law was responsible for changing people's opinions about alcohol, and more importantly, about the federal government's unwarranted involvement in the private lives of the American people.

Today, some of the very same arguments are being used in the "war on drugs."

22ND AMENDMENT

Proposed on March 24, 1947, and ratified on February 27, 1951, the Twenty-second Amendment was proposed by people who didn't want to see Franklin D. Roosevelt serve a fourth term. They wanted to limit the time presidents served in office to two terms. Furthermore, any president who served more than half of another president's term—such as for a president who either resigned or died—could only serve one full term after that one.

Early presidents George Washington and Thomas Jefferson both declined a third term, believing it was in the best interest of the nation to control the oligarchic nature of government to limit the time served on principle alone.

Since Franklin D. Roosevelt, only two presidents—Dwight D. Eisenhower and Ronald Reagan—have served two full terms.

23rd AMENDMENT

Proposed on June 16, 1960, and ratified on March 29, 1961, this amendment gave the citizens of Washington, D.C., the right to vote for president and vice president, and gave the District of Columbia three electoral votes. It did not, however, enable them to vote for members of the Senate or the House of Representatives (Congress).

24th AMENDMENT

Proposed on August 27, 1962, and ratified on January 23, 1964, the Twenty-fourth Amendment forbids the government from denying any citizen the right to vote in federal elections for refusing to pay a "poll tax," a tax required from all citizens at voting time, and which generally discouraged the poor and blacks from voting.

The amendment did not, however, prohibit individual states from requiring poll taxes in state elections, though the Supreme Court eventually ruled it unconstitutional and a violation of the Fourteenth Amendment.

25th AMENDMENT

Proposed on July 6, 1965, and ratified on February 10, 1967, the Twenty-fifth Amendment reiterated what Article

2 of the Constitution outlined, which was a disability clause for the presidency. It held that the vice president should "discharge the powers and duties of the presidency in case of the president's death, resignation, or inabilities." Up until that point, this clause hadn't been upheld—President James Garfield had laid in a coma for two months after an attempted assassination in 1881, and President Woodrow Wilson had suffered from a stroke between 1919–1921 without any substitution. Likewise, any vacancy in the vice presidency had, until then, remained that way until the following election. The Twenty-fifth Amendment merely sharpened what had already been constitutionalized.

It states that if the president dies or resigns, then the vice president automatically becomes president. If there becomes a vacancy in the vice presidency, then the president and Congress jointly appoint a new one. Finally, if for some reason the president becomes ill and the vice president stands in as acting president, Congress must decide when the president is well enough to come back to work—the president must get a "doctor's note" from Congress before resuming his or her duties in office.

In 1973 President Richard M. Nixon appointed Gerald R. Ford to the vice presidency after Vice President Spiro T. Agnew resigned. Then, on December 19, 1974, Nixon resigned and Ford became president, and Nelson A. Rockefeller became vice president. This was the first time that the United States had a president and vice president who had not been elected to office.

In recent history, starting on July 13, 1985, Vice President George Bush temporarily filled in for President Ronald Reagan for nearly three weeks, while Reagan underwent surgery for cancer.

26TH AMENDMENT

*P*roposed on March 23, 1971, and ratified on July 1, 1971, the Twenty-sixth Amendment was the fastest to ever be ratified. Earlier, by a swing vote decision in the Supreme Court case of *Oregon v. Mitchell,* the court ruled that Congress could not set an age limit in federal elections, but that it could in state elections. This amendment sets the legal voting age at eighteen for all citizens in federal, state, and local elections.

27TH AMENDMENT

*P*roposed in 1789, and ratified in 1992, the Twenty-seventh Amendment took the longest time to ever be ratified. The Twenty-seventh Amendment limits the number of pay raises Congress can grant itself. It does not, however, limit the *amount* of each raise. Some say this was a meager attempt by the federal government to place limitations and restrictions upon itself for face value.

28TH AMENDMENT

*T*here isn't one yet, but by the time this book is published, there's no telling what the 104th Congress might ratify. Some predict this is reserved for the flag burning amendment.

INDEX

A

abolition of slavery, 72-74
Agnew, Spiro T., 80
Ain't Nobody's Business If You Do, 52
American Civil Liberties Union (ACLU), 60
American Revolution, 14
anarchist, 5, 6, 8
Anthony, Susan B., 76
Articles of Confederation, 13, 14
assumption of innocence, 34, 50

B

Bill of Rights, 7, 10, 17, 18, 25, 57, 70, 73
Boston Massacre, 13
Boston Tea Party, 14
Brady Bill, 26, 27, 64
Brady, James, 26
British Parliament, 10
Bureau of Alcohol, Tobacco, and Firearms (BATF), 34
Burr, Aaron, 71
Bush, George, 80

C

check and balance, 70, 76

Chrisholm v. Georgia, 7
Civil War, 30, 72-74
"Common Sense," 14
communist, 7, 9
Confederacy, 72
Confederation, 15
confiscating property, 29, 35, 38-41
Congress, 14-17, 19, 31, 68, 70, 72-76, 78, 79, 80
congressional pay raises, 80
conservative, 7, 9
Constitution, 3, 4, 9, 15-18, 22, 26, 34, 37, 42, 47, 58, 59
Continental Congress, 13
criminal trial, 38, 42, 43
cruel and unusual punishment, 51, 52-57

D

damages in excess of twenty dollars, 48, 49
Davis, Jefferson, 63
Declaration of Independence, 3, 14, 15
Democrat, 6-8, 74
disability of president, 80
District of Columbia, 79
Douglas, Justice William O., 19

Drug Enforcement Agency (DEA), 34
due process of law, 37-39

E
Eighteenth Amendment, 76
Eighth Amendment, 51-57
Eisenhower, Dwight D., 79
Eleventh Amendment, 71
Emancipation Proclamation, 72
excessive bail, 51, 52

F
fascist, 7, 9
Federal Bureau of Investigation (FBI), 34
federal law, 26, 56, 64, 65, 66, 67, 68, 77
Fifteenth Amendment, 74
Fifth Amendment, 37-42
First Amendment, 3, 19-23
flag burning, 70, 81
Ford, Gerald R., 80
founders, 4, 8, 13-15, 23, 69, 70
Fourteenth Amendment, 73
Fourth Amendment, 33-36
Franklin, Benjamin, 14, 33
freedom of religion, 20
freedom of speech, 3, 19, 20-22
freedom of the press, 19, 20
French and Indian War, 13

G
grand jury, 38
group rights, 9, 10, 61

H
Hancock, John, 14
Hinckley, John, 26
House of Burgesses, 12
House of Representatives, 16, 17, 70-72, 79
housing of soldiers, 30-32

I
income tax laws, 74
individual rights, 1, 2, 4-10, 14, 25-29, 38, 39, 41, 43, 44

J
Jefferson, Thomas, 1, 14, 71, 78
July 4, 1776, 14
jury selection, 44
just compensation, 37-39, 41

L
lame duck, 77
liberal, 7-9
libertarian, 7, 9
life, liberty, and the pursuit of happiness, 3, 12, 37, 72
Lincoln, Abraham, 69, 72
Locke, John, 59
Los Angeles Times, 55, 60

M
Machiavelli, Nicolò, 24
Madison, James, 17, 69
mandatory sentence, 53, 54
mandatory drug test, 60
mandatory helmet law, 66, 67
McWilliams, Peter, 52
Mill, John Stuart, 58
moderate, 7-9

N
National Center for Policy Analysis, 55
Nietzsche, F. W., 51
Nineteenth Amendment, 76
Ninth Amendment, 58-62
Nixon, Richard M., 80

O
Oregon v. Mitchell, 80

P

Paine, Thomas, 14
political correctness, 21
poll tax, 79
Pollack v. Farmers' Loan, 74
preamble to the Constitution, 15
president, 16, 68, 71, 74, 77-79, 80
presidential term limit, 78
private property, 29, 34-37, 39-41, 60
prohibition, 76-78

R

race, color, or previous condition of servitude, 75, 78
ratification of amendments, 17, 70, 71-81
Reagan, Ronald, 26, 79, 80
Republican, 6-8, 72, 74, 75
retained rights, 58, 49, 62
right to a speedy, public trial, 43, 44, 46, 47
right to an attorney, 43
right to confront accuser, 45, 46
right to own guns, 4, 25, 28, 29, 34
right to privacy, 35, 60
right to vote, 12, 74, 76, 79
Rockefeller, Nelson A., 80
Roosevelt, Franklin D., 78, 79

S

search and seizure, 33-36, 77
Second Amendment, 4, 24-29, 62
self-incrimination, 38
Senate, 16, 17, 70, 72, 75, 77
Seventeenth Amendment, 75
Seventh Amendment, 48
Simpson, O. J., 34
Sixteenth Amendment, 75
Sixth Amendment, 43-47
state immunity, 71
state law, 44, 53, 72, 77
state legislatures, 17, 70
states' rights, 64, 73, 77
Story, Justice Joseph, 30
Supreme Court, 16, 35, 60, 61, 71, 75, 79, 81

T

taxes, 10, 13-16, 63, 74
Tenth Amendment, 63-68
Third Amendment, 30-32
Thirteenth Amendment, 72
Thoreau, H. D., 37
totalitarianism, 6-10
trial by jury, 14, 48-50
Tucker, Benjamin, 48
Twain, Mark, 43
Twelfth Amendment, 71
Twentieth Amendment, 76
Twenty-eighth Amendment, 81
Twenty-fifth Amendment, 79
Twenty-first Amendment, 77
Twenty-fourth Amendment, 79
Twenty-second Amendment, 78
Twenty-seventh Amendment, 81
Twenty-sixth Amendment, 81
Twenty-third Amendment, 79

U

Union, 72-74

V

vice president, 16, 71, 79, 80
victimless crimes, 52, 54
violent crime, 27, 54, 56
Voltaire, 10

W

Washington, George, 13, 14, 78

ABOUT THE AUTHOR

SHANNON FALLON WAS BORN IN NEW YORK AND HAS LIVED IN Southern California since the age of five. She is a graduate of the University of California at Irvine, and is currently in graduate school at California State Fresno. She is now living in Fresno with her husband, Paul, and their two labradors, Kato Clouseau and Jackson Browne.